Scienti

Albe

CW00384321

Mary Joseph

with Love
from Avani ben

ii sterling

STERLING PRESS PRIVATE LIMITED

Published by
STERLING PRESS PRIVATE LIMITED
A-59, Okhla Industrial Area, Phase - II, New Delhi-20
Tel: 26386165; Fax: 91-11-26383788
E-mail: ghai@nde.vsnl.net.in
Website: www.sterlingpublishers.com

Printed at Sterling Publishers (P) Ltd., New Delhi-110020

To my father, Abraham, a dedicated social worker and yet a man of personal reserve; much like Einstein who reflected that his own great reserve stood in curious contrast to his passionate interest in social responsibility.

In far-away Germany

Ulm was a small town in far-away Germany. In this town lived Hermann and Pauline Einstein. Mr Einstein owned a small company. Electricity had just been discovered and people all over Europe and America were putting electric lights in their houses. Mr Einstein's company supplied electrical equipment to people.

Hermann and Pauline were a happy couple. March 14, 1879 was a happy and exciting day for them because their son was born on this day. They named him Albert. Pauline loved her little boy. She held him

close to her and observed him with wonder. Mothers observe their babies very closely. They check to see if they are growing the right way. As Albert grew, he seemed to have a problem. He had not started speaking. Though his mother was very worried, she did not give up hope. His father thought that Albert was a dull baby. Little did he know that his son would grow up to be a genius the world would recognise.

When Albert was two years old, his sister Maja was born. Albert adored his baby sister.

"How tiny she is!" he exclaimed when he first saw her, "and so beautiful! I want to be her friend forever." And so it was to be throughout their lives.

Little Albert did not make friends easily. He was a quiet and shy boy. He did not care to play with the children of the neighbourhood. He hated the roughness and noise of their games. Children are gentle and innocent. Unfortunately they seem to delight in war-

games. Perhaps it is because they imitate what they see around them. You must imitate only what is good.

In Munich, where his parents had moved, the most popular game among children was playing at being soldiers. The children loved to join the military parades that passed the streets of Munich. But it was different with Albert. On seeing the soldiers he would begin to cry. He felt sorry for them. "When I grow up, I don't want to be one of those poor people," he would say to his father. He did not admire soldiers as other children did. In fact, he pitied them.

"Dad, these soldiers are like machines. They have no freedom," said Albert to his father, as he stood watching the parade. To him, freedom meant everything and so did peace. Later, as an adult, he fought for peace as Gandhi did, the non-violent way.

And so little Albert kept to himself. He spent his time day-dreaming or playing by himself games that needed a lot of thought and patience. Maja, very often, was part of this. Albert always loved, and looked forward to, the outings his parents planned for the family every Sunday. He would sit on the banks of the river and look with wonder at the rolling hills ahead and the great sky above. These trips created, in Albert's mind, an everlasting love for nature and a longing to understand how the universe worked.

One Sunday morning

One particular Sunday was special. It was Albert's birthday. He had turned five.

"Maja, I wonder what my birthday gift is going to be," said the excited Albert eagerly. He was so excited that he had woken up early and had woken Maja too. He had to share his excitement with her. Just then his parents walked in.

"Happy birthday, darling. Look what we have for you."

Opening the box, Albert saw something round and shiny. It was a magnetic compass.

He was fascinated. He could not take his eyes off it. What caught his attention most was the magnetic needle, that always pointed straight north. No matter which way he turned the compass, the needle would always point north. Why? How? So many questions came to Albert's mind as he gazed at the compass. "O thank you, Mum and Dad. This is such a wonderful gift! I'll treasure it forever," said the excited Albert.

That day, as Albert walked the hills by the river, he had many questions, for which he had no answers as yet.

Each morning, Albert woke to the strains of music. Pauline Einstein was a gifted pianist and so everyday the Einstein house was filled with music. She hoped that her children would absorb some of it. She believed that music was important to life. It made life beautiful.

So at six years of age, Albert began to learn the violin. His mother saw that music delighted him. It filled him with joy.

Music was always to be a part of his life. When he was older, he was greatly impressed by the writings of Solomon, a wise man in the Bible. The Bible is the holy book of Christians and Jews. After reading what Solomon had written, he himself wrote, and set to music, songs in praise of God. Even after he became a great scientist, trying to understand the universe, his violin would accompany him wherever he went.

Born to be free

Nowadays, whenever I see three-year-olds crying as they are forced inside school gates, I think of little Albert, who never really looked forward to school. To Albert school seemed a very military place. It reminded him of the times when he watched soldiers parade the streets of Munich. For him, school was a place which did not allow freedom. And freedom of thought, especially, was very important to Albert. He could not accept statements his teachers made, unless he understood them. Sometimes when he asked his teacher questions about Algebra, which the teacher could not answer, the teacher would get furious with him and punish him.

Apart from being too intelligent for his teachers, Albert had another problem. He was a Jew.

Now why should that be a problem, you may ask.

Unfortunately, there are no reasons for such problems. It is just that people sometimes like to be cruel. If most of the people in a country belong to one group, they sometimes make life miserable for the few who belong to another group. The people in Germany were mainly Christian. And, as I said, Albert was a Jew. Very often he was teased and insulted by other children on his way to school. This made him feel that he did not belong there. So next time try not to make another child feel left out, even if he does not belong to your group.

Being excluded left a deep impression on Albert's mind. It made him keep more to himself.

But he did make one very important childhood friend, surprisingly much older than himself. It was a Jewish custom to invite a poor Jew to dinner once a week. The Einstein family followed this custom. Every Thursday, Max Tamley, a medical student, was invited to their home for dinner. Max brought Albert many books on science.

"What lovely pictures, Max!" exclaimed Albert, as he glanced through the books. The pictures made him ask Max many questions. As he grew older, he read the books in great detail and discussed them with Max. They fascinated him and sharpened his mind. Max talked to him about science and philosophy. "What is philosophy, Max?" asked the curious Albert.

"Philosophy is the study of the meaning of life and the universe," said Max. The thirteen-year-old Albert began to think about things he had never thought about before.

"Max, how does the universe work?" asked Albert one day.

Max did not know the answer. He could not keep up with the way Albert's mind developed. Albert questioned ideas which people had already accepted. He knew that there was more to be learned about space and time. And since at that time he could not travel into space to find the answers, he started travelling in his mind. When he grew up, physics was to be his subject. It is a science which studies the physical world.

Dear Uncle Jake

Mr Einstein's brother Jacob lived with the family. He was a trained engineer. Albert was very fond of Uncle Jake. It was he, and not the teachers in school, who got Albert to love mathematics. One day he took Albert for a walk in the hills

"Albert, you love animals, don't you?" asked Uncle Jake.

"Why, yes," said the puzzled boy.

"Well, Algebra has many unknown animals in it. We have to try and find them."

"Really? How do we do that?" questioned Albert.

"When the animal that we're hunting can't be caught, we call it X, and continue hunting it, till it is caught."

"That sounds interesting. I want to learn more about it."

"That's enough for today. It's time to go back home," said Uncle Jake, who knew how to keep up the child's interest.

Albert's home was indeed an ideal place for his mind to develop. It was here that his real education took place. His father encouraged curiosity and discovery. He did not hinder these by being very strict with him, or by placing great importance on whether or not he got a good rank in class.

One winter's day when Albert returned home from school he had a surprise waiting for him.

"Look what I got for you," said his father, as Albert walked in.

"What is it, Dad?" asked the excited Albert as he fumbled with the wrapped gift.

It was a little book on geometry. It contained Euclid's ideas on the subject. Euclid was an ancient mathematician from Alexandria, in Egypt. This book enchanted Albert.

When Albert was about fifteen, his father faced serious problems with his factory. He had to finally close it down.

"Albert, I have some bad news for you," said his father one day. "I have to move to Milan, in Italy to earn money for all of us. I'm afraid you cannot come with us. You must remain in Munich to complete your studies at the Gymnasium."

"Oh, Dad, must I do that?" protested Albert. "You know how much I hate the Gymnasium. They never allow us any freedom. It is like a military place. Besides which I don't like being alone. I want to be with the family."

Unfortunately, very often we have to do things we do not like. Learning to do these things is part of growing up. Albert had to grow up. He had to finish his studies at the Gymnasium. The Gymnasium was the German school of the highest grade. Here students were prepared for the university.

Albert was so unhappy at the Gymnasium, after his parents left, that he could not concentrate on his studies. He was finally allowed to join them in Italy. Italy held Albert's interest. With its concerts, museums, and buildings steeped in art and culture, there was so much to see, to read and to think about. This was one of the happiest times of Albert's life.

Albert earns a degree

At sixteen, Albert went to Switzerland to attend a school at Aarau. Here he lived with the Winteler family. Mr Winteler was a teacher at the school. Very often Albert accompanied the Winteler family on long trips to the Swiss mountains. With them he developed a lasting friendship and later his sister Maja married Paul, Mr Winteler's son.

It was during this year that Albert become seriously interested in physics. He had an excellent teacher and he also was able to experiment in the school laboratory. While

studying here he asked himself, "What will happen if a man tries to catch a ray of light?" This question later led to his work on *relativity*.

It was believed by most scientists of that time that ether, an invisible substance, filled space. Young Albert was not prepared to accept this idea, as it had not been proved.

Albert joined the Swiss Federal Institute of Technology in Zurich and got his degree in physics.

'At last I can teach,' he thought. 'I want to be a different kind of teacher, not like the ones at the Gymnasium in Munich.' But alas! It was not to be as he wished it to be. The teachers felt threatened by Albert's superior intelligence. So they refused him a job. Finally when he was twenty-three, he got a job in Bern, the capital of Switzerland. He got a position at the Swiss patent office. He also got enough spare time to write many scientific papers. With determination he

worked at a Ph.D. He was finally awarded the degree and could now teach at the university.

When Albert was appointed as professor at the University of Zurich, people recognised him as a great scientist. Around that time, two American scientists, Michelson and Morley tried to measure the speed of light. They could not. Einstein said that they were unsuccessful because in truth, the speed of light always remains the same. Everything else in the universe is comparable or relative.

You must have learnt about comparisons when you were toddlers. To a man standing at a railroad crossing, a train moving at 90 kilometres per hour is very fast. But to a man, in a train, travelling at 120 kilometres per hour, the first train would appear to be moving very slowly. Einstein is famous for his *theory of relativity.*

A new approach to science

Isaac Newton was also a great scientist. He lived before Einstein. He had said that time always remained the same.

Einstein showed that time was relative, in his paper on the special theory of relativity.

The *theory of relativity* changed scientific thought with new ideas of time, space, motion and gravitation. His famous equation $E=mc^2$, which arose from this theory, led to the making of the atom bomb.

In one of his papers, Einstein suggested that light could be thought of as a stream of

tiny particles. This paper laid the basis for the 'electric eye'. This device made possible sound motion pictures, television and many other inventions. Einstein received the Nobel Prize in physics for this paper.

The whole world praised Einstein. They honoured him because he had so much knowledge. In spite of all this, Einstein remained humble. He treated all men equally. He gave the same respect to the president of a country as he did to the woman who cleaned his laboratory. Now that's true greatness! Einstein was a great admirer of Mahatma Gandhi who also worked for equality and peace among men.

Often as you sit in class listening to your teacher, you may have found it difficult to concentrate on what she is saying. Perhaps it is because other children are talking, or perhaps you are not interested in the subject at all. Einstein had great power of concentration. He was also greatly interested in the subject he was studying. He thought about his work everywhere. Once he stood on a bridge, waiting for his friend. His friend arrived late.

"I'm awfully sorry I kept you waiting, Albert," he said.

"There's no need to be sorry," responded Albert, "I was doing my work. I can do it anywhere – on a bridge, in a bathtub, or at the dinner-table." In fact, one day he scared his sister Maja by not coming out of the bathroom for a long time.

"Albert, is anything the matter?" asked his frightened sister as she knocked on the door frantically.

"I am sorry," said Albert as he came out of the bathroom. "I was working on a problem and I thought that I was sitting at my desk."

Einstein had become so famous that many centres of scientific research wanted him to be part of their centre. Kaiser Wilhelm of Germany had set up a research institute.

'Kaiser', means emperor, in German. Einstein was invited to be part of this institute.

A new life in America

A few years later Hitler was getting to be very powerful in Germany. Hitler hated the Jews. Einstein was a Jew and sensing great danger, he decided to leave Germany. The United States invited him to their country and so he left Germany in 1933.

When Einstein landed in New York, photographers and reporters rushed to him. But Einstein never made great of his fame. In fact, he made jokes about it. "The ladies in New York want to have a new style each year. This year the fashion is relativity," he said.

Nevertheless, he did make use of his fame. He used it to help those people who were treated unjustly and he used it to fight for peace. Writers, educators, scientists, artists and entertainers guide the thoughts of people. They cannot remain silent since their responsibility is greater. Though Einstein was silent and reserved by nature, he was never silent about this responsibility. He knew that people would listen to him because he was famous. So he made full use of his fame. As a result, many people were helped.

Einstein admired Gandhi, the frail, little man because of whom the great British Empire bowed out of India. When Nehru and Indira Gandhi visited Einstein, he praised the non-violent methods used by Gandhi to win independence. He felt that when nations competed with each other, the result was war. All his life he fought for friendship and peace.

But one thing he regretted all his life. Owing to Einstein's scientific research, scientists later discovered the atom bomb. But because it was mainly his research that showed the way to the making of the bomb, he has often been referred to as the father of the atom bomb. When the Japanese cities of Hiroshima and Nagasaki were bombed and destroyed, Einstein could not get this tragedy out of his mind. He worked all the more for peace and brotherhood among people.

A horse for single harness

It is strange that in spite of being concerned about people and doing much to uplift them, Einstein could never be close friends with anyone. He described himself as a "horse for single harness". He could never really be part of a team.

Einstein felt that to be happy we must never be attached to people and things – we must only work towards our goal. His goal was to understand the universe. It always made him marvel at it. It was something beyond his understanding. He felt that it was

when man stood in wonder, that he was capable of great art and science. His work opened the door to the universe. These days scientists study the universe because it was made possible by Einstein's work.

Albert Einstein always loved children. He respected them too as much as he respected presidents and other important people. He talked seriously with them, listening to their ideas and discussing the ideas with them. In the quiet college town of Princeton, Einstein was a familiar sight as he walked each day from his home to his office. On the way, he greeted children and babbled with babies. He loved to show them that he could wiggle his ears. This always made them laugh. Seeing him regularly without any socks, one little girl warned him that his mother would be annoyed with him, as he would catch cold. Einstein loved these comments from little children. He once wrote to them:

"Bear in mind that the wonderful things that you learn in your schools are the works of many generations. All this is put into your hands as your inheritance in order that you may receive it, honour it and add to it."

Einstein received, honoured and added to the knowledge handed over to him by the scientists of old. It is our turn now.